Contents

Introduction	**5**
TA1 Pre-conception health and reproduction	**6**
1.1 Factors affecting pre-conception health for women and men	6
Recall activities	6
Short-answer exam-style practice questions	7
1.2 Other factors affecting pre-conception health for women	8
Recall activities	8
Short-answer exam-style practice questions	9
1.3 Types of contraception methods and their advantages and disadvantages	10
Recall activity	10
Short-answer exam-style practice questions	12
1.4 The structure and function of the reproductive systems	14
Recall activities	14
Short-answer exam-style practice questions	16
1.5 How reproduction takes place	17
Recall activities	17
Short-answer exam-style practice questions	18
1.6 The signs and symptoms of pregnancy	20
Recall activity	20
Short-answer exam-style practice questions	20
Long-answer exam-style practice questions	21
TA2 Antenatal care and preparation for birth	**25**
2.1 The purpose and importance of antenatal clinics	25
Recall activities	25
Short-answer exam-style practice questions	28
2.2 Screening and diagnostic tests	30
Recall activities	30
Short-answer exam-style practice questions	32
2.3 The purpose and importance of antenatal (parenting) classes	33
Recall activity	33
Short-answer exam-style practice questions	34
2.4 The choices available for delivery – hospital or home	35
Recall activity	35
Short-answer exam-style practice questions	36
2.5 The role of the birth partner in supporting the mother through pregnancy	37
Recall activity	37
Short-answer exam-style practice questions	37
2.6 The methods of pain relief when in labour	38
Recall activity	38
Short-answer exam-style practice questions	39
2.7 The signs that labour has started	40
Recall activity	40
Short-answer exam-style practice questions	40

2.8 The three stages of labour and their physiological changes	**41**
Recall activity	41
Short-answer exam-style practice questions	42
2.9 The methods of assisted birth	**42**
Recall activity	42
Short-answer exam-style practice questions	43
Long-answer exam-style practice questions	**44**

TA3 Postnatal checks, postnatal care and the conditions for development — 47

3.1 Postnatal checks	**47**
Recall activities	47
Short-answer exam-style practice questions	48
3.2 Postnatal care of the mother and baby	**50**
Recall activities	50
Short-answer exam-style practice questions	52
3.3 The developmental needs of children from birth to five years	**53**
Recall activities	53
Short-answer exam-style practice questions	55
Long-answer exam-style practice questions	**56**

TA4 Childhood illnesses and a child-safe environment — 59

4.1 Recognise general signs and symptoms of illness in children	**59**
Recall activities	59
Short-answer exam-style practice questions	61
4.2 How to meet the needs of an ill child	**61**
Recall activities	61
Short-answer exam-style practice questions	62
4.3 How to ensure a child-friendly safe environment	**64**
Recall activities	64
Short-answer exam-style practice questions	67
Long-answer exam-style practice questions	**68**

Introduction

This workbook will help you to prepare to tackle exam questions for your Cambridge National in Child Development (J809) exam: Unit R057 Health and well-being for child development.

The exam lasts for 1 hour and 15 minutes and is worth 70 marks. The exam has two sections:
- **Section A** is worth 40 marks and includes scenario-based short, medium and extended response questions. One question will be an extended response question worth 8 marks.
- **Section B** is worth 30 marks and question types may include short and medium answer, multiple-choice questions and extended responses. Questions in this section will not be based on scenarios or situations.

You will be tested on the following topic areas:
- Topic Area 1: Pre-conception health and reproduction
- Topic Area 2: Antenatal care and preparation for birth
- Topic Area 3: Postnatal checks, postnatal care and the conditions for development
- Topic Area 4: Childhood illnesses and a child-safe environment

Questions may focus on one topic area or might require answers that combine information from two or more topic areas.

Features to help you succeed

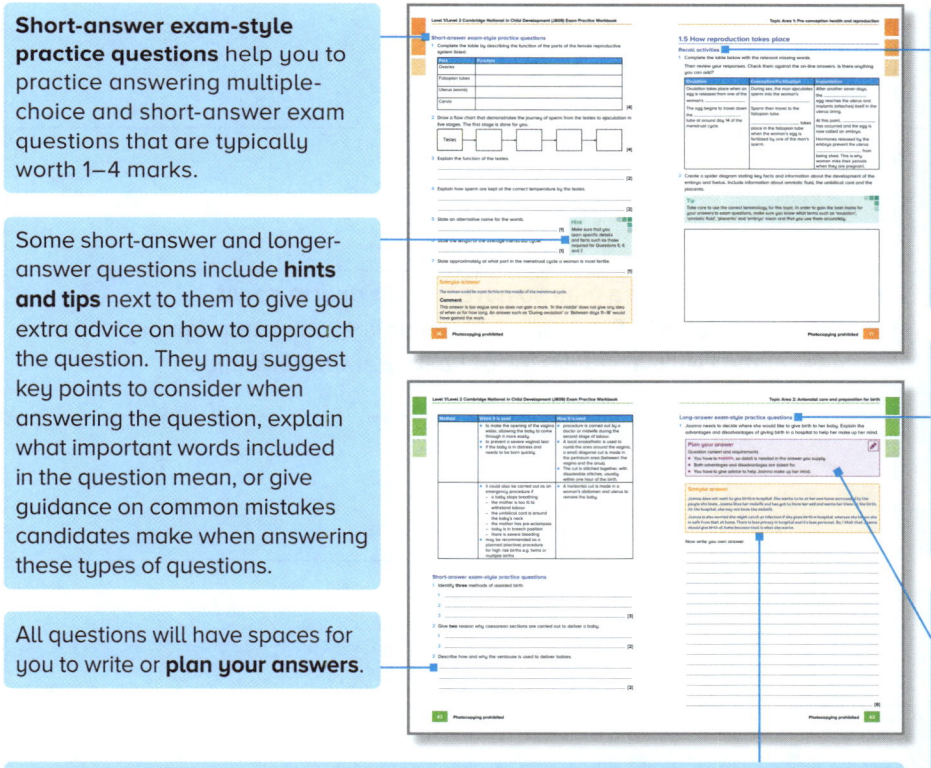

Short-answer exam-style practice questions help you to practice answering multiple-choice and short-answer exam questions that are typically worth 1–4 marks.

Some short-answer and longer-answer questions include **hints and tips** next to them to give you extra advice on how to approach the question. They may suggest key points to consider when answering the question, explain what important words included in the question mean, or give guidance on common mistakes candidates make when answering these types of questions.

All questions will have spaces for you to write or **plan your answers**.

Example student answers or extracts from student answers are provided for some questions. These will help you understand how to gain the most marks and may ask you to think about the strengths and weaknesses of the answer and how it could be improved.

Each topic area starts with **recall activities** that will help you to remember important information you will need when answering exam questions. These activities include crosswords, quizzes, matching exercises and filling in missing words in tables, sentences or diagrams.

Longer-answer exam practice questions will help you to practice answering extended-response questions typically worth 6–9 marks. These questions will usually include a context or scenario.

Some questions will also include a series of stages or activities to support you as you answer the question. They may identify and explain key words for you, have headings, bullet points or mind maps for you to complete to help you to plan and structure your answer or include partially completed answers.

Answers to all the questions are available online at www.hoddereducation.co.uk/cambridgenationals-2022/answers

Topic Area 1: Pre-conception health and reproduction

Hints

Pre-conception means the period of time before a woman gets pregnant.

Pre-conception health involves consideration of health, fitness and lifestyle <u>before</u> trying for a baby, to improve the chances of becoming pregnant and to give the baby a good start.

1.1 Factors affecting pre-conception health for women and men

Recall activities

1 Fill in the table below with examples of the possible effects of each factor affecting pre-conception health. Try to think of at least two effects for each factor.

Tip
Know the meaning of the key terms.

One of these has been done for you.

Factors affecting pre-conception health	Effects on pre-conception health
Weight	
Smoking	
Drinking alcohol	• Alcohol may cause a man to have a lower sperm count. • Drinking alcohol before conception (for both men and women) is associated with a higher risk of heart defects in babies.
Taking recreational drugs	
Parental age	

2 Complete these sentences.

    a Smoking can be .... to someone trying to conceive.

    b Alcohol can .... fertility for someone trying to conceive.

Topic Area 1: Pre-conception health and reproduction

Short-answer exam-style practice questions

1 Fill in the table below by ticking whether each statement is **true** or **false**.

Statement	True	False
Smoking is known to reduce fertility for both men and women.		
Being underweight or overweight/obese can affect a woman's ovulation and so reduce fertility.		
Drinking alcohol does not affect male fertility.		
Men remain fertile longer than women.		

[4]

2 Identify **two** factors that could have a negative effect on male fertility.

1 ....

2 .... [2]

3 Explain why men remain fertile longer than women.

....

....

.... [2]

> **Sample answer**
>
> The man may have more sperm.
>
> **Comment**
>
> This answer would gain one mark, as it is a little vague. More detail in the answer, such as 'men produce sperm, and so remain fertile for their whole adult life', would gain the second mark.

4 State **three** facts about a woman's age that can affect her fertility.

1 ....

2 ....

3 .... [3]

1.2 Other factors affecting pre-conception health for women

Recall activities

1 Choose the correct immunisations from the list below to complete the table. Write **one** immunisation only in each box.

- Rubella/MMR
- Coronavirus (COVID-19)
- Whooping cough
- Flu
- HPV
- Meningitis

> **Tips**
> - You need to learn the names of the immunisations and why it is important to have them.
> - You could use a highlighter to identify key information on the table when answering this question. This will help you to refer to the main information quickly because the key points will stand out.

Name of immunisation	Reason for having the immunisation
	Pregnant women are more likely to get flu complications than women who are not pregnant, and are more likely to be admitted to hospital. This vaccine is recommended.
	Most babies with this condition will be admitted to hospital. Ensuring the mother has this vaccine during pregnancy, at any stage after 16 weeks, also ensures that she produces antibodies that pass on to the baby, giving them some protection until they have their own vaccination at 8 weeks old.
	If pregnant, a woman is at greater risk of being seriously ill if they catch this virus. If it is late in the pregnancy, the baby could also be at risk. It is safe to have the vaccine at any stage of pregnancy. It is not recommended to delay it until after the birth.
	Most women will have had this vaccine as a child. It is not recommended to be given to pregnant women. If given in the first three months of pregnancy it can cause birth defects. So, it is important to be up to date beforehand and to have had the vaccine well in advance of pregnancy.

Topic Area 1: Pre-conception health and reproduction

2 Complete a folic acid fact sheet with information for each of the three headings.

Folic acid fact sheet
When a folic acid supplement should be taken:
Reasons folic acid is needed:
Folic acid should be taken along with a diet of folate-rich foods such as:

Short-answer exam-style practice questions

1 Give **three** reasons why it is important to take folic acid during pregnancy.

   1 ....

   2 ....

   3 .... [3]

2 Give **one** example of when a woman should start to take folic acid.

   .... [1]

3 State **four** sources of folic acid, other than oral supplements.

   1 ....

   2 ....

   3 ....

   4 .... [4]

4 State **one** reason why the MMR immunisation is not recommended during pregnancy.

   .... [1]

5 Explain why it is important to have the whooping cough immunisation during pregnancy.

....

....

.... [3]

6 Explain what can happen during pregnancy if the pregnant mother does not have the flu vaccine.

....

....

.... [3]

> **Sample answer**
>
> *Pregnant women can easily get complications if they get flu.*
>
> **Comment**
>
> This is a correct answer and gains one mark for identifying that complications can occur.
>
> The answer could be further developed by stating that pregnant women are more likely to develop serious complications that can lead to them being admitted to hospital. This would gain a higher mark.

1.3 Types of contraception methods and their advantages and disadvantages

Recall activity

1 Create at least **two** revision cards of different contraceptive methods. A completed example is shown below.

Male condoms	
These are made from latex; polyurethane condoms are available for men with a latex allergy. The condom is put on to the erect penis before it comes into contact with the vagina. Condoms are designed to prevent pregnancy by stopping the sperm from meeting an egg.	
Advantages	Disadvantages
98% effective if used correctly	if not used properly, male condoms can slip off or split, limiting their effectiveness
protect against STIs including HIV	single-use only and then discarded
easily obtained – sold widely at pharmacies, supermarkets	the penis has to be quickly withdrawn from the vagina after ejaculation
available free from most family planning or sexual health clinics	having to plan ahead/have one available to use

Topic Area 1: Pre-conception health and reproduction

Your cards should include the name of the method, a description of how it is used and give the advantages and disadvantages of the method. Choose methods from **two different** columns in the table below.

Barrier methods	Hormonal methods	Natural family planning	Other

• Male condoms
• Female condoms
• Diaphragm or cap
	• Contraceptive pills:
	  – combined pill
	  – progesterone-only pill (POP)
	• Contraceptive injection
	• Contraceptive implant
	• Intrauterine system
	• Emergency contraceptive pill
		• Temperature
		• Cervical mucus method
		• Calendar method
			• Intrauterine device (non-hormonal)

Name of Method:

Description of method:

Advantages	Disadvantages

Name of Method:

Description of method:

Advantages	Disadvantages

Level 1/Level 2 Cambridge National in Child Development (J809) Exam Practice Workbook

Short-answer exam-style practice questions

1 Explain how the male condom prevents pregnancy.

> **Sample answer**
>
> A male condom is placed onto an erect penis before coming into contact with the vagina. Any sperm released will be caught in the condom, preventing the sperm going into the vagina.
>
> **Review this answer**
>
> - Use the mark scheme to mark this sample answer.
> - Put a tick by each correct point and a cross for any errors (if any).
> - How many marks did you give?
> - Is it a good explanation? Why or why not?

Write a review of the sample answer here.

....

....

Mark scheme

Answer	Marks	Guidance
How a male condom prevents pregnancy: • The condom covers the erect penis • It is made from latex, which provides a barrier • It is put onto the erect penis before it comes into contact with the vagina • Use of spermicide helps kill the sperm • The condom prevents the sperm from entering the vagina/catches the sperm • The condom prevents sperm from reaching the egg • It prevents fertilisation/prevents sperm reaching the fallopian tubes	3	**Three** marks for an explanation that covers any three of the points listed

Now write your own answer.

....

....

....

.... [3]

> **Hint**
>
> - You should write answers to exam questions, like this **explain** question, in sentences.
> - If the question requires a **list** or to **state**, you can give one-word answers.

12 Photocopying prohibited

Topic Area 1: Pre-conception health and reproduction

2 Three weeks ago Jenna had unprotected sex and now thinks she might be pregnant as she has missed a period.

   a State **one** method of contraception that Jenna could have used after having unprotected sex.

   .... [1]

   b Identify **one** advantage and **one** disadvantage of this method of contraception.

   Advantage: ....

   Disadvantage: .... [2]

3 Explain how long it can take for fertility to return to normal after the contraceptive injection wears off.

   .... [1]

4 Identify **one** advantage and **one** disadvantage of using the diaphragm (cap) as a method of contraception.

   Advantage: ....

   Disadvantage: .... [2]

5 State **three** hormonal methods of contraception.

   1 ....

   2 ....

   3 .... [3]

6 Explain how a female condom works.

   ....

   ....

   ....

   .... [3]

7 State **one** advantage and **one** disadvantage of using a female condom.

   Advantage: ....

   Disadvantage: .... [2]

1.4 The structure and function of the reproductive systems

Recall activities

1 Complete the table with the name and an explanation of the function of each part of the female reproductive system. The first one has been completed for you.
Use the diagram of the structure of the female reproductive system to help you.

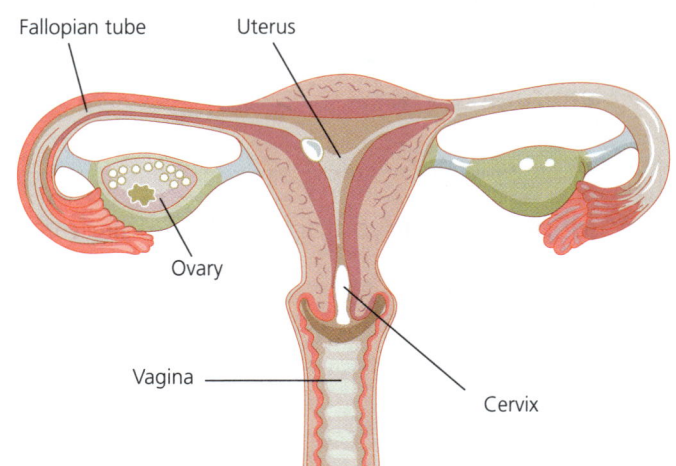

Main parts of the female reproductive system	Function
Ovaries	A woman has two ovaries. They contain hundreds of undeveloped egg cells called ova and release one egg a month. This is called 'ovulation'. The ovaries control the production of hormones - oestrogen and progesterone.

2 Using information in the diagram below, explain what happens at each of the four stages of the menstrual cycle.

Stage 1 ....
....
....

Stage 2 ....
....
....

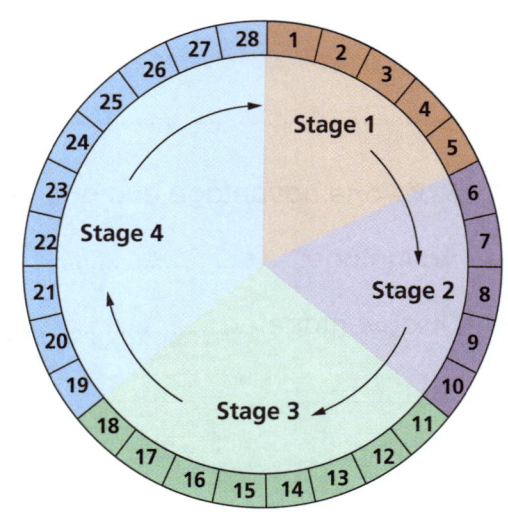

Topic Area 1: Pre-conception health and reproduction

Stage 3 ....

....

Stage 4 ....

....

3 Complete the second column in the table with an explanation of the function of each part of the male reproductive system. The first one has been completed for you.

Use the diagram of the structure of the male reproductive system to help you.

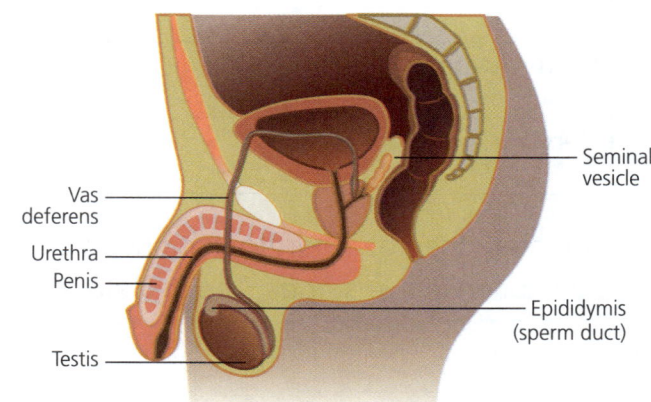

Main parts of the male reproductive system	Function
Testes	There are two testes. They are also known as testicles. They produce sperm and the male hormone testosterone. The testes are in the scrotum, which is a sac of skin behind the penis. The sac is outside the body to keep the sperm at the best temperature.
Epididymis (sperm duct)	
Seminal vesicle	
Vas deferens	
Urethra	
Penis	

Photocopying prohibited 15

Short-answer exam-style practice questions

1 Complete the table by describing the function of the parts of the female reproductive system listed.

Part	Function
Ovaries	
Fallopian tubes	
Uterus (womb)	
Cervix	

[4]

2 Complete the flow chart to demonstrate the journey of sperm from the testes to ejaculation in five stages. The first stage is done for you.

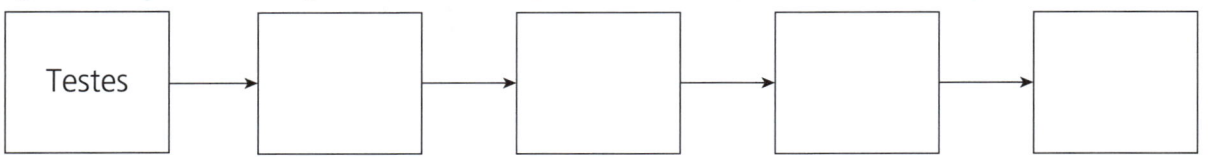

[4]

3 Explain the function of the testes.

....

.... [2]

4 Explain how sperm are kept at the correct temperature by the testes.

....

.... [2]

5 State an alternative name for the womb.

.... [1]

6 State the length of the average menstrual cycle.

.... [1]

> **Hint**
> Make sure that you learn specific details and facts such as those required for Questions 5, 6 and 7.

7 State approximately at what part in the menstrual cycle a woman is most fertile.

.... [1]

> **Sample answer**
>
> The woman would be most fertile in the middle of the menstrual cycle.
>
> **Comment**
>
> This answer is too vague and so does not gain a mark. 'In the middle' does not give any idea of when or for how long. An answer such as 'During ovulation' or 'Between days 11–18' would have gained the mark.

1.5 How reproduction takes place

Recall activities

1 Complete the table below with the relevant missing words.

Then check your responses against the online answers. Is there anything you can add?

Ovulation	Conception/Fertilisation	Implantation
Ovulation takes place when an egg is released from one of the woman's ……………………… The egg begins to travel down the ……………………… tube at around day 14 of the menstrual cycle.	During sex, the man ejaculates sperm into the woman's ……………………… Sperm then travel to the fallopian tube. ……………………… takes place in the fallopian tube when the woman's egg is fertilised by one of the man's sperm.	After another seven days, the ……………………… egg reaches the uterus and implants (attaches) itself in the uterus lining. At this point, ……………………… has occurred and the egg is now called an embryo. Hormones released by the embryo prevent the uterus ……………………… from being shed. This is why women miss their periods when they are pregnant.

2 Create a spider diagram stating key facts about the development of the embryo and foetus. Include information about amniotic fluid, the umbilical cord and the placenta.

> **Tip**
> Take care to use the correct terminology for this topic. In order to gain the best marks for your answers to exam questions, make sure you know what terms such as 'ovulation', 'amniotic fluid', 'placenta' and 'embryo' mean and that you use them accurately.

3 The table below is incomplete. Insert the points below into the relevant column.

o These twins develop when two eggs are released and each is fertilised by a different sperm.

o They can be either the same sex, or a boy and a girl.

o These twins result when one fertilised egg splits into two parts.

> **Tip**
> Make sure you can **explain** the difference between identical and non-identical twins.

Identical twins	Non-identical/fraternal
• Each part of the fertilised egg develops into a separate individual • The twins will be very similar in appearance • They are always of the same sex as they have inherited identical genes • • •	• The chance of having non-identical twins increases with the age of the woman • The twins will be no more alike than any other two children in the same family • There may be a history of twins in the woman's family • • •

Short-answer exam-style practice questions

1 Complete the information below using the words provided.

placenta   **amniotic**   **umbilical**   **nutrients**

This is a protective fluid, mainly water, called .... fluid. It cushions the baby's movements inside the womb. This is where water, ... and antibodies are transferred between the mother and her baby.

The .... cord is a tube that connects the foetus to the mother throughout the pregnancy. Blood flows through the umbilical cord to and from the .... The baby's blood comes very close to the mother's but does not mix. [4]

2 Describe what happens when ovulation takes place.

....

....

.... [2]

Topic Area 1: Pre-conception health and reproduction

3 Explain what conception means and where it takes place.

....

....

.... [2]

4 Explain the process of implantation.

....

....

....

.... [3]

> **Model answer**
>
> After the egg is fertilised, it travels through the fallopian tube until it arrives at the uterus. The fertilised egg then fixes or 'implants' in the lining of the uterus. Conception has occurred and the egg is now an embryo. This is how the implantation process happens.
>
> **Comment**
>
> This is a good answer. It is factually correct and written in an organised way that demonstrates understanding. It covers the process of implantation and gains three marks.

5 Identify approximately at which point in the menstrual cycle a woman is most fertile.

.... [1]

6 State **one** purpose of the umbilical cord.

.... [1]

1.6 The signs and symptoms of pregnancy

Recall activity

1 The table below describes the five main signs and symptoms of pregnancy.

Choose from the list of symptoms below to complete the first column of the table. One example has been done for you.

- Passing urine more frequently than usual
- Tiredness
- Feelings of nausea and vomiting
- Breast changes

Signs and symptoms of pregnancy	
	Becoming larger, feel heavier and may even feel sore
	Nipples may be darker and stand out more
Missed period	Often the first and most common sign. It is the most reliable sign for someone who has a regular menstrual cycle
	Often called 'morning sickness' but can occur at any time, not just in the morning
	Early on in pregnancy this is due to hormonal changes. Later it is caused by the pressure of the growing uterus on the bladder
	Due to hormone changes in the body to begin with. Later it can be the additional weight being carried and lack of sleep

> **Tip**
> Avoid thinking that 'morning sickness' only happens in the morning. It does not – it can happen at any time of day or night.

Short-answer exam-style practice questions

1 What can cause tiredness and the passing of urine more frequently early in pregnancy?

.... [1]

2 State **one** cause of tiredness and lack of sleep towards the end of pregnancy.

.... [1]

3 Is a missed period always a reliable sign of pregnancy? Give **two** reasons for your answer.

....

....

.... [2]

Topic Area 1: Pre-conception health and reproduction

4 Describe how breasts can change early in pregnancy.

....

....

....

....

.... [4]

Model answer

Many women find that their breasts feel similar to when they have a period, that is, feeling tender and becoming slightly larger. Additionally, when pregnant, veins may appear darker and more noticeable than usual. Some women feel a tingling, along with tenderness. The nipples may also be affected, becoming darker and standing out more than usual.

Comment

This answer gains the full four marks. Each of the changes are described in some detail and are factually accurate. The command verb of the question is 'describe' and the student has successfully done this and covered the main changes accurately. If this answer had been a simple list of four changes, then fewer marks would have been gained.

Long-answer exam-style practice questions

1 Explain how men can ensure good pre-conception health when planning to start a family.

Give **two** factors.

Plan your answer

Question context and requirements:
- the question context is pre-conception health
- the focus is on men
- two factors should be explained — therefore reasons must be included within your answer.

Sample answer

Men should give up smoking if at all possible if they want to start a family. Research has shown that smoking can lower a man's sperm count; this can reduce the chances of getting the woman pregnant as there are less sperm. Smoking can also cause male smokers the risk of a higher proportion of abnormal sperm. Having abnormal sperm increases the chance of a baby being conceived with abnormalities. The same applies to being overweight.

Review the sample answer

- Does it cover pre-conception health for men?
- Does it explain two factors for good pre-conception health?
- Use the mark scheme to mark the model answer. How many marks did you give it? Why?
- Can you suggest anything extra to make a stronger answer?

Mark scheme

Answer	Marks	Guidance
Explanation points can include: **Weight** - Need to follow healthy eating guidelines - Maintain a healthy weight - Avoids risk of low sperm count - Low sperm count can cause difficulties conceiving - Research indicates that men who are overweight or obese have reduced quality sperm and significantly lower sperm counts than men of healthy weight **Smoking** - Lowers sperm count = difficulty conceiving - Male smokers risk a higher proportion of abnormal sperm - Abnormal sperm increases the chance of baby having abnormalities **Alcohol/drugs** - Men who drink alcohol can have a lower sperm count - Consuming alcohol/taking drugs can lead to permanent infertility due to poor sperm quality and quantity	8	**Level 3: 6–8 marks** - Thorough explanation showing detailed understanding of two factors for ensuring good pre-conception health for men - Makes relevant points that are developed - Uses appropriate terminology **Level 2: 3–5 marks** - Adequate explanation showing sound understanding of one or two factors for ensuring good pre-conception health for men - Makes relevant points, some of which are developed - Uses some appropriate terminology **Level 1: 1–2 marks** - A brief explanation which shows limited understanding of one or two factors for ensuring good pre-conception health for men - Points made may not be relevant - Little or no use of appropriate terminology **Note:** Credit can be given for any other appropriate response.

Now write your own answer.

....

....

....

....

....

....

....

....

....

.... **[8]**

Topic Area 1: Pre-conception health and reproduction

2 Describe the function of the placenta in the development of the foetus.

> **Sample answer**
>
> The placenta helps to deliver nutrients to the baby. These will help it grow and develop organs, etc. Another way the placenta helps is by transferring blood to and from the baby. The blood carries oxygen and helps with the baby's development. The placenta also helps with getting rid of waste produced by the foetus.
>
> **Review the sample answer**
>
> - Use the mark scheme to mark the sample answer. How many marks did you give?
> - Put a tick by each correct point and a cross for any errors (if any).
> - Is it a good description? Why or why not?

Mark scheme

Answer	Mark	Guidance
Description points can include: **Function of the placenta** - Placenta is the organ through which the baby feeds while in uterus/it provides nutrients - Placenta is the organ through which the baby breathes while in the uterus - Placenta is the organ through which the baby excretes waste while in the uterus - The placenta passes on antibodies – creating natural/passive immunity **Development of the foetus** - Baby's and mother's blood are close enough for food and oxygen to pass from mother to baby and for carbon dioxide and waste products from the baby's kidneys to pass from foetus to mother - Blood from baby flows continually to and from the placenta through the umbilical cord - In the placenta, the baby's blood comes very close to the mother's blood but <u>does not mix</u> - The foetus needs oxygen and nutrients to develop in the uterus, which the placenta provides - The foetus needs waste substances removed via the placenta	6	**Level 3: 5–6 marks** - Answers will provide a detailed description of the function of the placenta related to the development of the foetus - Answers will be clear and logically structured - Answers use appropriate terminology **Level 2: 3–4 marks** - Answers will provide some description of the function of the placenta with some reference to the development of the foetus - Answers are presented with some structure and are relevant - Uses some appropriate terminology **Level 1: 1–2 marks** - Answer provides basic/limited description of the function of the placenta, with little or no reference to the development of the foetus - Answers may be list-like, muddled, demonstrating little knowledge or understanding - Little or no use of appropriate terminology **Note:** Credit can be awarded for any other appropriate response.

> **Tip**
>
> - The topic is the function of the placenta linked to the development of the foetus.
> - A description is required, so details are needed, not just a list.
> - To check your knowledge, you could create a spider diagram of facts to use in your answer.
> - Structure your answer by writing in paragraphs – this helps with organising your response.

Now write your own answer.

....

....

....

....

....

....

....

....

....

.... [6]

> **Review your own answer**
> - Mark your answer using the mark scheme. What mark would you give your answer? Why?
> - Does it clearly describe the function of the placenta?
> - Does it link with the development of the foetus?
> - Is the answer organised? Have you used paragraphs? Have you drifted off the topic at all?
> - Can you suggest anything extra, if needed, to strengthen the answer?

Topic Area 2: Antenatal care and preparation for birth

Topic Area 2: Antenatal care and preparation for birth

Hint
Antenatal care is the care someone will receive from health professionals while pregnant. In the term 'antenatal', 'ante' means 'before' and 'natal' relates to birth.

2.1 The purpose and importance of antenatal clinics

Recall activities

1 Complete the missing information using the words provided.

sickle cell disease   screening   nutrition   ten weeks   drinking alcohol

Timing of the first antenatal clinic appointment:

The first midwife appointment should happen before ....

This is because some routine tests should be done by then, such as testing for

.... or thalassaemia.

The mother will be given information about folic acid supplements, ...,

diet and food hygiene and lifestyle factors (such as smoking, ...

and recreational drug use), antenatal .... and diagnostic tests.

2 Fill in the chart with examples of the GP, midwife and obstetrician roles in pregnancy care. Some examples have been done for you to get you started. Try to include **at least three more** for each role.

GP	Midwife	Obstetrician
• Will answer initial questions and give initial advice on pregnancy to the mother	• Will help create a birth plan	• Has appointments with the pregnant woman if there are complications with the pregnancy
• Will discuss any existing medical conditions the mother may have that could affect her pregnancy	• Gives advice on healthy eating and exercise for a healthy pregnancy	• Will deliver the baby if there are any complications
•	•	•
•	•	•
•	•	•

Photocopying prohibited

3 Complete the spider diagram to show further reasons for conducting routine tests during pregnancy

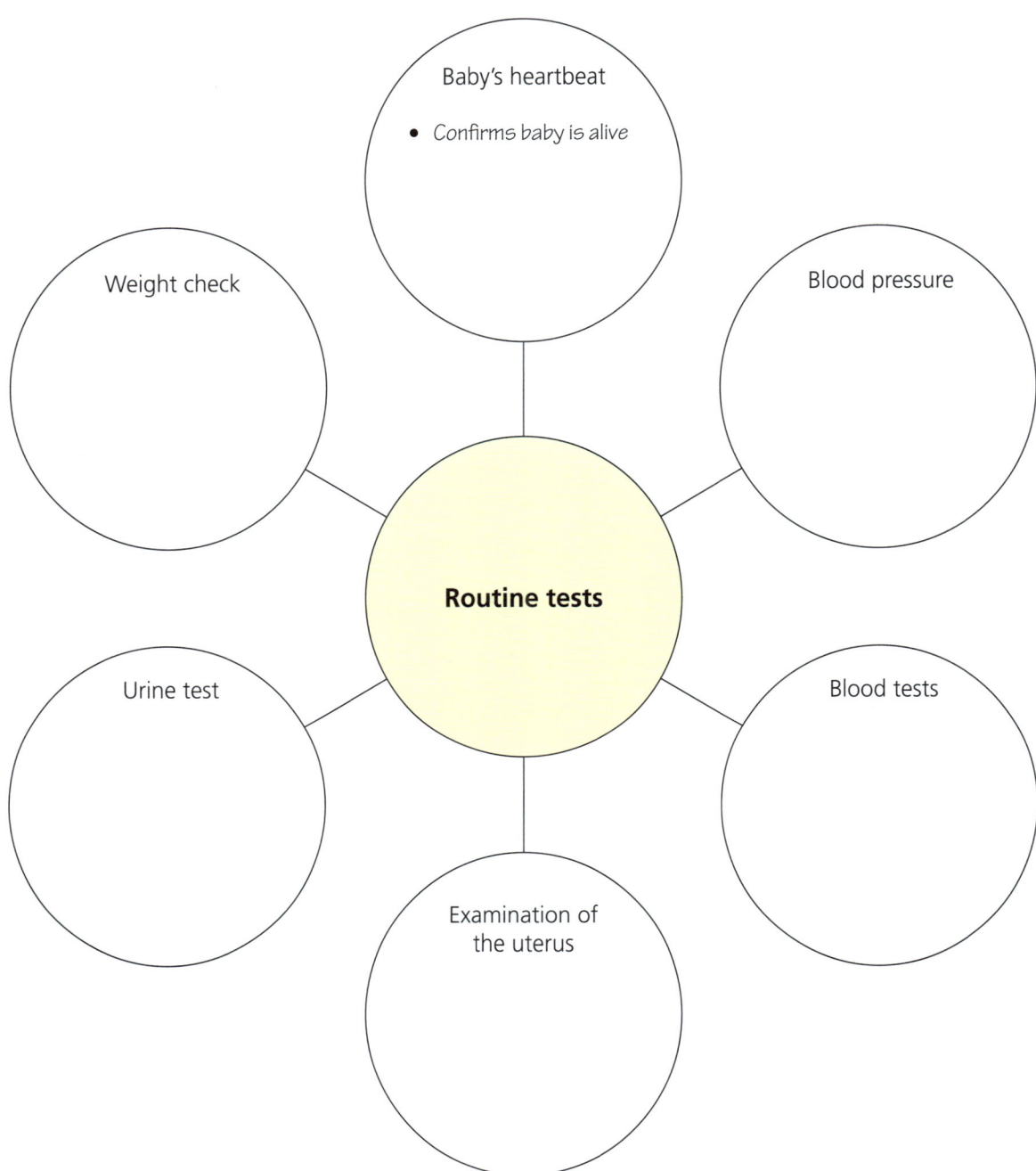

Topic Area 2: Antenatal care and preparation for birth

4 When preparing for labour and childbirth, a birth plan is desirable. The plan covers arrangements for pain relief, location of the birth and immediate post-birth requirements.

Add options to the birth plan template below to provide the expectant mother with the ability to present her choices to the midwife. The first section has been completed for you.

<u>**My Birth Plan**</u>

How and where I would like to give birth
- ☐ Home birth
- ☐ Hospital birth
- ☐ Water birth
- ☐ Natural lighting if possible
- ☐ Dim lights
- ☐ Music of my choice playing
- ☐ Aromatherapy
- ☐ Minimal interruption/Quiet environment
- ☐ With my birth partner
- ☐ No students observing

Pain management
- ☐ ....
- ☐ ....

Comfort during labour
- ☐ ....
- ☐ ....
- ☐ ....
- ☐ ....

Labour and pushing
- ☐ ....
- ☐ ....
- ☐ ....
- ☐ ....
- ☐ ....
- ☐ ....

After birth
- ☐ ....
- ☐ ....

Feeding
- ☐ ....
- ☐ ....

Short-answer exam-style practice questions

1. What is sickle cell disease?

   ....

   .... [1]

2. State the meaning of thalassaemia.

   .... [1]

3. State **one** reason why a baby's heartbeat is checked.

   .... [1]

4. Give **two** reasons why an examination of the uterus is carried out.

   1 ....

   2 .... [2]

5. Explain **two** reasons why a mother's weight is checked regularly.

   1 ....

   2 .... [2]

6. During her pregnancy Sam has been cared for by an obstetrician. Describe the role of an obstetrician.

   Use the mark scheme to mark the two student answers.

   > **Sample answer 1**
   >
   > It is a medical worker who gives advice for high-risk pregnancies. Helps you decide where to give birth.
   >
   > **Sample answer 2**
   >
   > An obstetrician specialises in dealing with complicated pregnancies, such as a multiple birth. They will also perform caesarean sections or use intervention methods such as forceps deliveries.
   >
   > **Review the two answers**
   > - Use the mark scheme to mark the sample answers.
   > - Put ticks next to up to three correct points and a cross for any errors.
   > - How many marks did you give?
   > - Why is one answer better than the other – what makes it a good answer?

   Write a review to compare the sample answers here.

   ....

   ....

   ....

Topic Area 2: Antenatal care and preparation for birth

Mark scheme

Answer	Guidance

Three marks for a description.
The role of an obstetrician:
● A doctor specialising in:
  – complicated deliveries
  – high-risk births
  – providing medical care to mothers during pregnancy
● Will see pregnant women if there are complications with the pregnancy
● Deals with multiple births
● Performs caesarean sections
● Uses intervention methods such as forceps and ventouse
	For description:
	3 marks:
	● Answer includes detail that clearly shows understanding of the role of an obstetrician
	● Three valid points provided
	2 marks:
	● Answer includes detail that shows some understanding of the role of an obstetrician
	● Two valid points included
	1 mark:
	● A basic statement or identification with no elaboration
	● One valid point included

Now write your own answer.

....

....

....

.... [3]

7 Layla attends an appointment at the antenatal clinic where the midwife carries out routine checks and tests. Fill in the right-hand column of the table to provide the name of each check described.

Use the mark scheme below to mark the two sample answers.

Sample answer 1

Description of a routine check	Name of the check
A check that indicates the size of the baby.	Uterus examination
A check that could be used to detect if the mother has anaemia.	Blood test
A check that could be used to detect if pre-eclampsia is a risk.	Urine test
A check that could show the baby has stopped growing.	Weight check

Sample answer 2

Description of a routine check	Name of the check
A check that indicates the size of the baby.	Weight check
A check that could be used to detect if the mother has anaemia.	Uterus examination
A check that could be used to detect if pre-eclampsia is a risk.	Blood test/urine test
A check that could show the baby has stopped growing.	Baby's heartbeat check

> **Review the two answers**
> - Use the mark scheme to mark the sample answers – if two answers are given for the same check, only the first one is marked.
> - Put ticks by correct answers and a cross for any errors.
> - How many marks did you give?

Write a review to compare the sample answers here.

....

....

....

Mark scheme

Answer			Guidance
Four marks for correct choices.			The number of ticks will match the number of marks awarded. For an **incorrect** answer, use a **cross**. **If more than one answer is written in the box**, only the first one is marked.
Description of a routine check	**Name of the check**		
A check that indicates the size of the baby.	Examination of the uterus		
A check that could indicate if the mother has anaemia.	Blood test		
A check that could indicate if pre-eclampsia is a risk.	Urine test		
A check that could show if the baby has stopped growing.	Weight check		

2.2 Screening and diagnostic tests

Screening and diagnostic tests are done to check the current health of the mother and baby, so that appropriate treatment, if needed, can be provided as early as possible.

Recall activities

1 There are two definitions below. One is for **diagnostic tests** and the other is for **screening tests**. Insert the name of the correct type of test in the boxes below.

Type of test	Definition
	These tests are carried out to diagnose and confirm whether or not an individual has a disease.
	These tests are carried out to estimate the level of risk of the baby being born with a particular disease or condition.

Topic Area 2: Antenatal care and preparation for birth

2 Complete the second column of the table with all you know about each type of ultrasound scan.

Use your textbook or the NHS website if you need to find more details.

Ultrasound scans	
Dating scan – 12 weeks	
Anomaly scan – 20 weeks	
Nuchal fold translucency scan	
Triple test	
Non-invasive pre-natal testing (NIPT)	

3 Complete the second column of the table with all you know about each type of diagnostic test.

Use the textbook or the NHS website if you need to find more details.

Diagnostic tests	
Amniocentesis	
Chorionic villus sampling (CVS)	

Tip
- Don't mix up 'screening' and 'diagnostic' tests. It is important to know the difference as they test for different things.
- Make sure you can give examples of conditions that each type of test is used to diagnose.

Short-answer exam-style practice questions

1 Explain the difference between diagnostic and screening tests.

   ....

   ....

   ....

   ....

   .... [4]

2 Name **two** diagnostic tests.

   1 ....

   2 .... [2]

3 Name **two** screening tests.

   1 ....

   2 .... [2]

4 State **one** reason for having an amniocentesis test.

   .... [1]

5 Identify **two** reasons for having a CVS (chorionic villus sampling) test.

   1 ....

   ....

   2 ....

   .... [2]

6 Ultrasound anomaly scans usually happen when the mother is between 18 and 21 weeks pregnant. Tick ✓ the name of the person who carries out this scan.

Person carrying out an anomaly scan	Tick ✓ the correct answer
Obstetrician	
Sonographer	
Anaesthetist	

[1]

2.3 The purpose and importance of antenatal (parenting) classes

Recall activity

1 Create a detailed spider diagram with information about the purpose and importance of antenatal (parenting) classes.

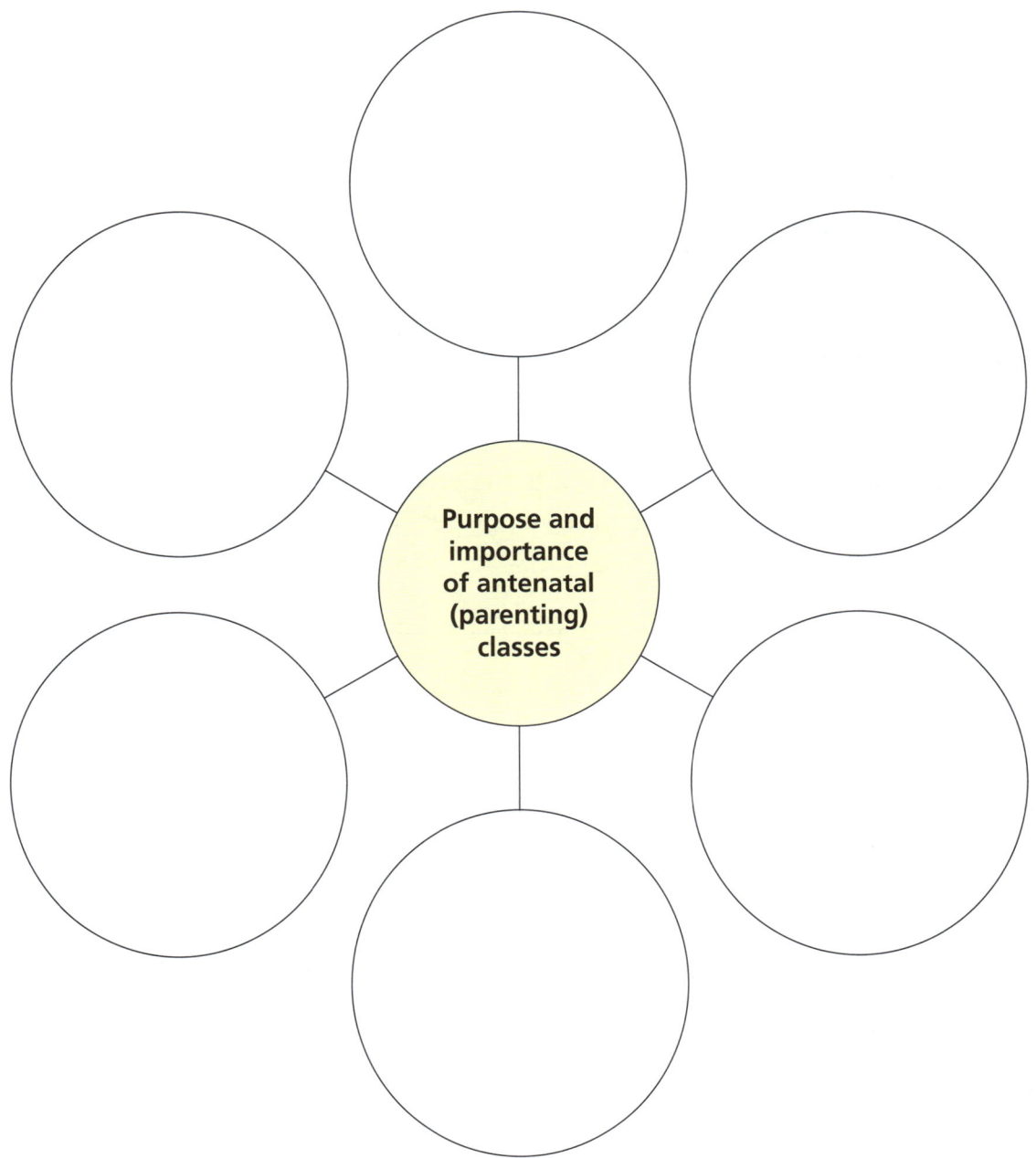

> **Tip**
> It is wrong to assume that antenatal and parenting classes are just for mothers. A partner, family member or a friend are always welcome to attend and support the prospective mother.

Short-answer exam-style practice questions

1 State **three** purposes of attending antenatal (parenting) classes.

   1 ....

   2 ....

   3 .... [3]

> **Sample answer**
>
> 1 To meet other people.
> 2 To learn about labour and birth.
> 3 Find out about pain relief.
>
> **Comments and additional guidance**
>
> This answer gains two marks. Answers 2 and 3 are good because they both give correct and very specific reasons. Answer 1 is very vague – what other people? The answer should specify how attending antenatal (parenting) classes is a good way to make friends with other parents who are expecting babies at around the same time. This puts the answer into context, rather than giving a vague reference to 'other people'.

2 A partner can attend antenatal classes with the pregnant woman. A partner may be the father of the child. Identify **three** alternative partners who could attend the classes with the pregnant mother.

   1 ....

   2 ....

   3 .... [3]

3 Antenatal classes will provide advice on feeding and caring for the baby. Give **three** examples of advice that could be provided.

   1 ....

   2 ....

   3 .... [3]

4 Explain why breast feeding is encouraged during the first two weeks of a baby's life.

   ....

   ....

   ....

   .... [4]

2.4 The choices available for delivery – hospital or home

Recall activity

1 Complete the **two** tables below with reasons for having a hospital or home birth. Then identify the advantages and disadvantages of both. Some examples have been included for you.

> **Tip**
> Be sure to give advantages and disadvantages for both home and hospital births.

Reasons for choosing a hospital birth
• The best choice if any complications have been identified.
•
•
•

Advantages of a hospital birth	Disadvantages of a hospital birth
• Expert, trained staff are available if there is a problem or emergency.	• Hospitals can be noisy, busy and not very relaxing.
•	•
•	•
•	•

Reasons for choosing a home birth
• Familiar surroundings can make the mother feel more relaxed and in control.
•
•
•

Advantages of a home birth	Disadvantages of a home birth
• The family can follow their own routine, not that of the hospital ward.	• Certain types of pain relief are not available at home, such as an epidural.
•	•
•	•
•	•

Short-answer exam-style practice questions

1 Identify **four** reasons why a hospital birth might be advised.

   1 ....

   2 ....

   3 ....

   4 .... [4]

2 State **two** reasons why an obstetrician would be involved in delivering a baby.

   1 ....

   2 .... [2]

3 Describe **two** advantages of a home birth.

   1 ....

   ....

   2 ....

   .... [2]

> **Model answer**
>
> The mother might feel more confident and relaxed being with her family at home. Hospitals can be very noisy with lots of people.
>
> It is likely that the midwife delivering the baby will have been the one the mother has been seeing throughout the pregnancy so they will know each other, which is very comforting.
>
> **Comment**
>
> This is an excellent answer. There is a clearly displayed understanding of the situation with relevant, accurate and detailed reasons provided. Full marks.

2.5 The role of the birth partner in supporting the mother through pregnancy

Recall activity

1 Complete the two tables below, filling each box with examples of the type of physical and emotional support a birth partner could provide through the pregnancy, labour and birth.

Physical support	Emotional support
• During labour, e.g. massaging the mother's back and shoulders • • •	• During labour, e.g. just being there so the mother does not feel alone • • •

> **Hint**
>
> **Physical support** means practical help – doing tasks for the pregnant, or new, mother, lifting the shopping, carrying things, cleaning, doing the washing, etc.
>
> **Emotional support** means help with feelings and emotions, giving her time to relax, providing reassurance, being actively involved in learning about pregnancy and birth, asking how they can help.

Short-answer exam-style practice questions

1 Describe the role of a birth partner and give **three** reasons why they are required.

   ....

   ....

   .... [3]

2 Identify **one** health professional seen at a first antenatal appointment.

   .... [1]

3 State **three** examples of physical support a birth partner could provide.

   1 ....

   2 ....

   3 .... [3]

4 State **three** examples of emotional support a birth partner could provide.

   1 ....

   2 ....

   3 .... [3]

2.6 The methods of pain relief when in labour

Recall activity

1 Create a set of cards, one for each of the following methods of pain relief used in labour.

   o gas and air (Entonox)   o pethidine   o TENS machine.

   Make sure you have described the method and listed the advantages and disadvantages.

   An example revision card is shown below.

Epidural anaesthetic

Description: This involves a tube being inserted in the lower back, by an anaesthetist, in hospital. The anaesthetic is administered through the tube and can be topped up when needed.

Advantages:	Disadvantages:
• gives complete pain relief • numbs the nerves that carry the pain impulses from the birth canal to the brain • can be helpful for a long or particularly painful birth • it does not usually cause any drowsiness or nausea	• can only be given by an anaesthetist • possible headache and backache • temporary loss of bladder control • not able to drive or drink alcohol for 24 hours afterwards • the numbness lasts a few hours before its effects wear off

---

Gas and air (Entonox)

Description:

Advantages:	Disadvantages:

Topic Area 2: Antenatal care and preparation for birth

Pethidine	
Description:	
Advantages:	Disadvantages:

TENS machine	
Description:	
Advantages:	Disadvantages:

Short-answer exam-style practice questions

1 Identify **one** drug-free form of pain relief that can be used in labour.

   .... [1]

2 Identify **one** form of pain relief used during labour that needs to be administered by an anaesthetist.

   .... [1]

3 Describe **two** disadvantages of pethidine when used as pain relief during labour.

   1 ....

   2 .... [2]

2.7 The signs that labour has started

Recall activity

1 Complete the table with signs that labour has started. The first column has been done for you. Add **three** points to each of the columns.

Show	Waters breaking	Contractions start
• A discharge or 'show' of blood-stained mucus	•	•
• Back ache or back pain	•	•
• Nausea, vomiting and/or diarrhoea	•	•

Short-answer exam-style practice questions

1 Identify **two** signs that labour has started.

   1 ....

   2 .... [2]

2 Describe the different types of contractions during labour.

   ....

   ....

   ....

   .... [3]

2.8 The three stages of labour and their physiological changes

Recall activity

1 Using the three boxes below, create a flow chart describing the three stages of labour and their physiological changes. The first stage has been completed for you.

Labour stage 1: Neck of the uterus opens
• This is the longest stage of labour – can last 15–18 hours • The contractions get stronger and more intense, more pain relief may be needed • The cervix gradually dilates to reach a width of 8–10 cm

↓

Labour stage 2: Birth of the baby

↓

Labour stage 3: Delivery of the placenta

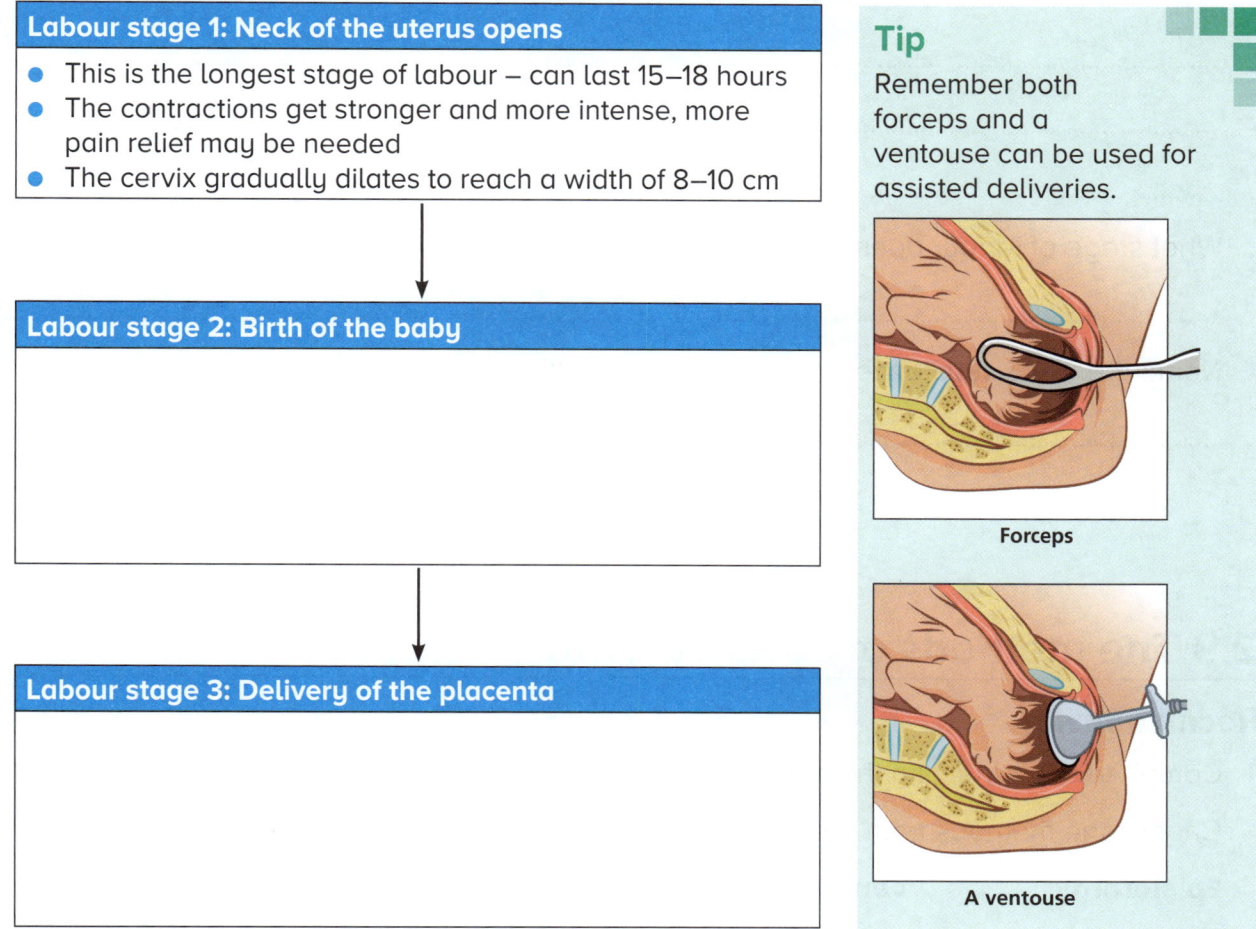

Tip

Remember both forceps and a ventouse can be used for assisted deliveries.

Forceps

A ventouse

2 The sentences below explain part of the second stage of labour. Insert the correct words from the list below to complete the sentences.

dilation   10 cm   canal   contractions   open   cervix

The second stage of labour starts when the .... becomes fully

.... and ends when the baby is born. When the cervix reaches

full .... at .... a passage is formed called the birth

.... help move the baby down the birth canal.

Short-answer exam-style practice questions

1 How many centimetres is a fully dilated cervix?

   .... [1]

2 Describe the physical changes that take place during the second stage of labour.

   ....

   ....

   ....

   .... [1]

3 What stage of labour does the placenta deliver?

   .... [1]

4 Name the white substance that covers babies after birth.

   .... [1]

2.9 The methods of assisted birth

Recall activity

1 Complete the table with the name of the correct method of assisted birth.

   Choose the methods from the list.

   Episiotomy **Ventouse** **Forceps** **Caesarean section**

Method	When it is used	How it is used
	• when there are concerns over baby's heart rate or if the baby is distressed • if baby is in an awkward position • if mother is too exhausted and too tired to push	• large metal tongs are placed around the baby's head • can help to turn the baby into the right position to be born • used by an obstetrician by gently easing the head out to help deliver the baby
	• when the contractions are not strong enough to push baby out and assistance is needed.	• this is a plastic or metal cap that fits on the baby's head • this is sometimes known as a 'suction cup' as it attaches to the baby's head by suction • as the mother pushes with each contraction, an obstetrician pulls to help deliver the baby

Topic Area 2: Antenatal care and preparation for birth

Method	When it is used	How it is used
	• to make the opening of the vagina wider, allowing the baby to come through it more easily • to prevent a severe vaginal tear • if the baby is in distress and needs to be born quickly	• procedure is carried out by a doctor or midwife during the second stage of labour. • A local anaesthetic is used to numb the area around the vagina, a small diagonal cut is made in the perineum area (between the vagina and the anus). • The cut is stitched together, with dissolvable stitches, usually within one hour of the birth.

	• it could also be carried out as an emergency procedure if
	  – a baby stops breathing
	  – the mother is too ill to withstand labour
	  – the umbilical cord is around the baby's neck
	  – the mother has pre-eclampsia
	  – baby is in breech position
	  – there is severe bleeding
	• may be recommended as a planned (elective) procedure for high risk births e.g. twins or multiple births
		• A horizontal cut is made in a woman's abdomen and uterus to remove the baby.

Short-answer exam-style practice questions

1 Identify **three** methods of assisted birth.

   1 ....

   2 ....

   3 .... [3]

2 Give **two** reason why caesarean sections are carried out to deliver a baby.

   1 ....

   2 .... [2]

3 Describe how and why the ventouse is used to deliver babies.

   ....

   ....

   .... [2]

Long-answer exam-style practice questions

1 Joanna needs to decide where she would like to give birth to her baby. Explain the advantages and disadvantages of giving birth in a hospital to help her make up her mind.

> **Plan your answer**
> Question context and requirements
> - You have to **explain**, so detail is needed in the answer you supply.
> - Both advantages and disadvantages are asked for.
> - You have to give advice to help Joanna make up her mind.

> **Sample answer**
>
> Joanna does not want to give birth in hospital. She wants to be at her own home surrounded by the people she loves. Joanna likes her midwife and has got to know her well and wants her there at the birth. At the hospital, she may not know the midwife.
>
> Joanna is also worried she might catch an infection if she gives birth in hospital, whereas she knows she is safe from that at home. There is less privacy in hospital and it's less personal. So, I think that Joanna should give birth at home because that is what she wants.

Now write you own answer.

....
....
....
....
....
....
....
....
....
....
....
....
.... [8]

Topic Area 2: Antenatal care and preparation for birth

> **Review your answer**
> - Look through the mark scheme for this question. How does your answer match up?
> - Mark your answer using the mark scheme
> - Note: the mark scheme states that a comparison with a home birth is not required – does the answer follow this instruction?
> - Do you think your answer would help Joanna to make her decision
> - What (if anything!) needs to be improved?

Mark scheme

Answer	Marks	Guidance
Advantages and disadvantages of giving birth in hospital **Advantages** - Mother may feel safer - Trained staff available if there is a problem - Specialist equipment available if needed for the baby - Only option if caesarean needed - Only option if forceps and ventouse needed - Some types of pain relief can only be given in hospital/wider range of pain relief available - Midwife available to answer any questions - No household responsibilities - Can meet other new mothers - More opportunities to rest/restricted visiting hours - Sterile conditions **Disadvantages** - Less privacy - Hospitals usually associated with illness/people are sometimes frightened by hospitals - Less personal - Father/birth partner may not be as involved with the birth - Possibility of picking up hospital-acquired infections, e.g. MRSA - Not always with the same midwife - Noisy/busy in hospital/not relaxing/lots of visitors Accept other appropriate points with explanation.	8	**Level 3: 6–8 marks** - Detailed explanation - At least two advantages and two disadvantages - Relevant and accurate information - Understanding of hospital birth is evident **Level 2: 3–5 marks** - Some explanation but not fully developed - May be unbalanced – one or two advantages OR disadvantages explained - Mostly relevant and accurate information **Level 1: 1–2 marks** - Little or no explanation - Information may be list-like/muddled - Limited advantages or disadvantages identified *Note:* A comparison with a home birth is *not* required.

2 Explain how attending antenatal and parenting classes could prepare the birth partner for labour and parenthood. Name **two** factors.

....

[6]

Topic Area 3: Postnatal checks, postnatal care and the conditions for development

3.1 Postnatal checks

Recall activities

1 Complete the two lists below with details of the purpose of vernix and lanugo.

Purpose of vernix:
- It is a natural moisturiser.
-
-

Purpose of lanugo:
- It keeps the baby's body at the right temperature.
-
-

2 The baby's weight, length and head circumference are measured after the birth. Complete the table below with reasons for these checks. One has been completed for you.

Postnatal check	Reasons for check
Weight	
Length	• Recorded on a centile chart (a graph that shows the expected pattern of growth of a healthy baby) so it can be checked regularly. • To check against the average length at birth, which is 50–53 cm.
Head circumference	

3 Complete the crossword below which covers the areas of the newborn baby's body where physical checks are made in the first five days of their lives.

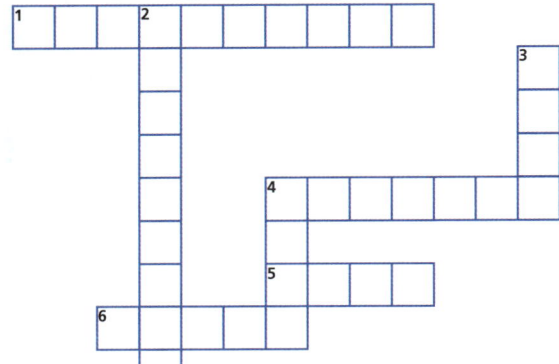

ACROSS
1 Soft area on the top of the baby's head (10)
4 Found at the end of the baby's hands (7)
5 Found on the baby's face (4)
6 Pumps the baby's blood around the body

DOWN
2 These are checked in male babies (9)
3 These are checked for mobility and any signs of clicking (4)
4 These are found at the end of the baby's legs (4)

4 Choose words from the list below to complete the sentences about the heel prick test.

prevent **blood** **conditions** **serious**

a Newborn blood spot screening involves taking a .... sample to find out if the baby has one of nine rare but .... health conditions.

b Most babies will not have any of these .... but, for the few that do, the benefits of screening are enormous.

c Early treatment can improve their health and .... severe disability or even death.

Short-answer exam-style practice questions

1 State **two** purposes of measuring a newborn baby's Apgar score immediately after the birth.

1 ....

2 .... [2]

2 State what the letters 'Apgar' stand for. **A** has been done for you.

A Activity — is the baby moving and active?

P ....

G ....

A ....

R .... [4]

Topic Area 3: Postnatal checks, postnatal care and the conditions for development

3 State the average weight and length of a newborn baby.

....

.... [2]

4 Explain why it is important to regularly check a baby's weight.

....

....

....

....

.... [4]

> **Tip**
> You don't need to remember all of the conditions tested for by the heel prick test – just two or three. However, you will need to know why the checks are carried out. Marks can be lost if you can only name the tests but cannot give reasons for the checks. Make sure you know why the checks are done.

5 Serena is unsure about taking her new baby to have the heel prick test. Explain to Serena why she should take her baby for the test.

....

....

....

....

.... [4]

6 Name **three** conditions that the heel prick test checks for.

1 ....

2 ....

3 .... [3]

7 Identify **two** physical checks that are carried out on a baby's eyes and fontanelle?

Give **one** answer for each.

Eyes: ....

Fontanelle: .... [2]

3.2 Postnatal care of the mother and baby

Recall activities

1 Create a detailed spider diagram with information about the role of the health visitor.

Topics could include providing information about vaccines and advice on all aspects of baby care and child care, including feeding and bath-time routines and safe sleeping.

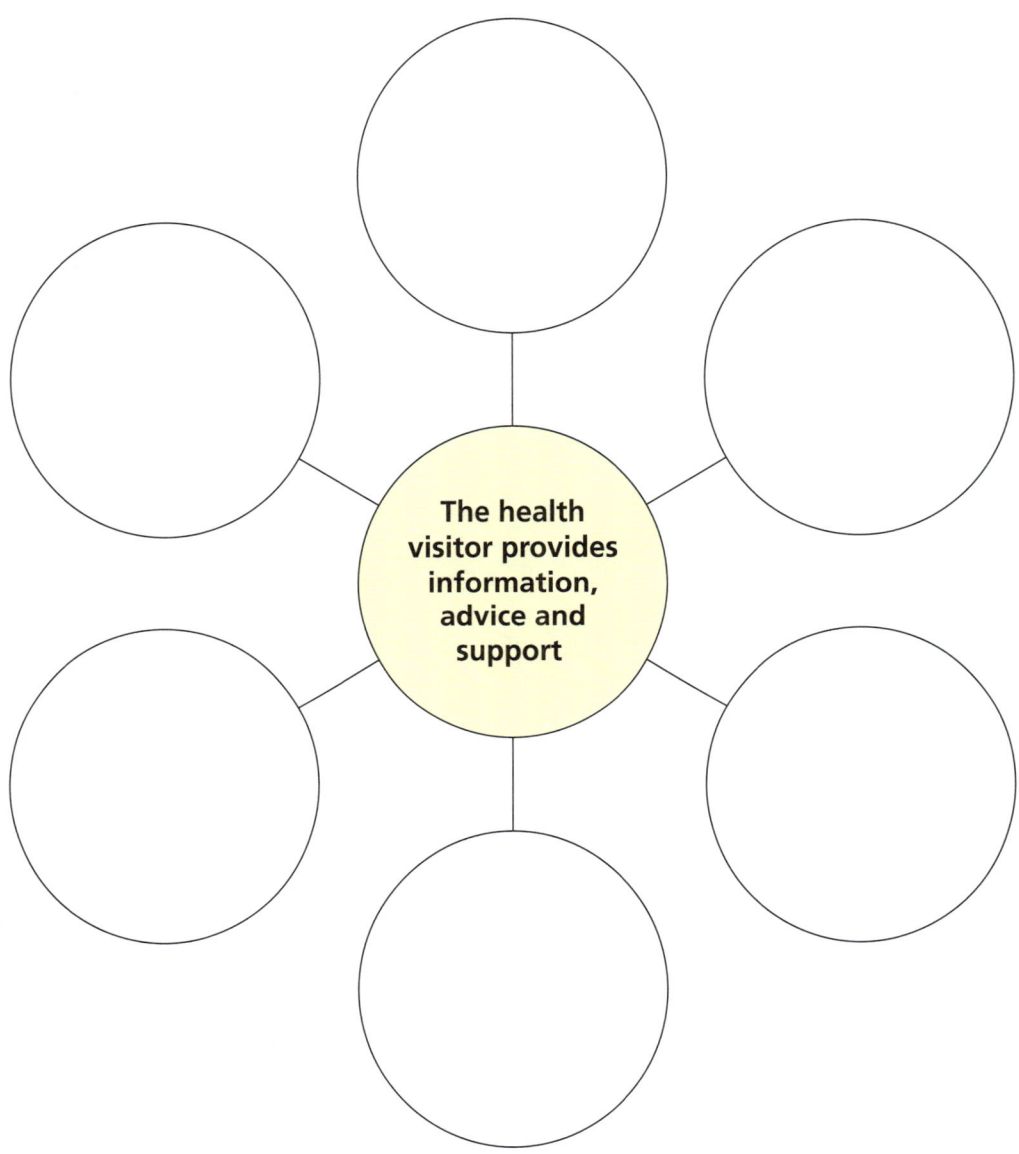

Topic Area 3: Postnatal checks, postnatal care and the conditions for development

2 Complete the table below with **four** 'Do's' and **four** 'Don't's' for safe sleeping and reducing the risk of SIDS.

An example for each has been completed for you.

> **Tip**
> Make sure you understand and can explain some advice to prevent Sudden Infant Death Syndrome (SIDS).

Do:	Do not:
Always place the baby on its back to sleep	Do not put the baby on its side or tummy to sleep

3 There are various ways the partner can provide physical and emotional support for the mother. Some of these are listed below.

Provide examples of how a partner can support a new mother. An example answer has been added to each column for you.

Physical support	Emotional support
• Bathing baby	• Be sympathetic and empathetic so she feels supported

4 Make a list of ways in which family and friends could provide physical and/or emotional help.

- Practical help with things like shopping
- Tell mother she is doing a great job — supporting her emotions
-
-
-
-
-
-

> **Hint**
> When answering a question about types of support, do not write that family members can 'look after baby'. You must write something more specific about what they could actually do, like 'bath the baby' or 'cook a meal'. These types of answers are required to gain marks.

5 Complete the following description to show what is usually covered at the six-week check using the words provided.

stitches   concerns   discussion   blood   weight   vaginal

- The mother is asked how she is feeling as part of a general .... about her mental health and well-being.
- She will be asked if she still has any .... discharge and whether she has had a period since the birth.
- Her .... pressure will be checked.
- She will be offered an examination to check if .... have healed (if she had an episiotomy or caesarean) and whether the uterus is going back to the correct size.
- Contraception will be discussed.
- The mother's .... will be checked – weight loss and healthy eating guidance will be given.
- The mother will be asked if she has any .... about herself or baby, sleeping, breast feeding, etc.

Short-answer exam-style practice questions

1 Identify what the initials SIDS stand for.

   .... [1]

2 Explain the safe sleeping position.

   ....

   ....

   .... [2]

3 Identify **four** pieces of advice for a mother that will reduce the risk of SIDS.

   1 ....

   2 ....

   3 ....

   4 .... [4]

4 State the purpose of the six-week check.

   ....

   .... [2]

Topic Area 3: Postnatal checks, postnatal care and the conditions for development

5 Isabelle visits her GP for her six-week postnatal check. Identify **four** routine checks the GP will carry out.

1 ....

2 ....

3 .... [4]

6 State **three** concerns a new mother should always tell the GP about.

1 ....

2 ....

3 .... [3]

7 State **two** symptoms of postnatal depression.

1 ....

2 .... [2]

3.3 The developmental needs of children from birth to five years

Recall activities

1 Create **two** revision cards. Choose **two** of the development needs from the list below and complete the tables on the next page. Make sure you describe the importance of the need being met, and how it can be met.

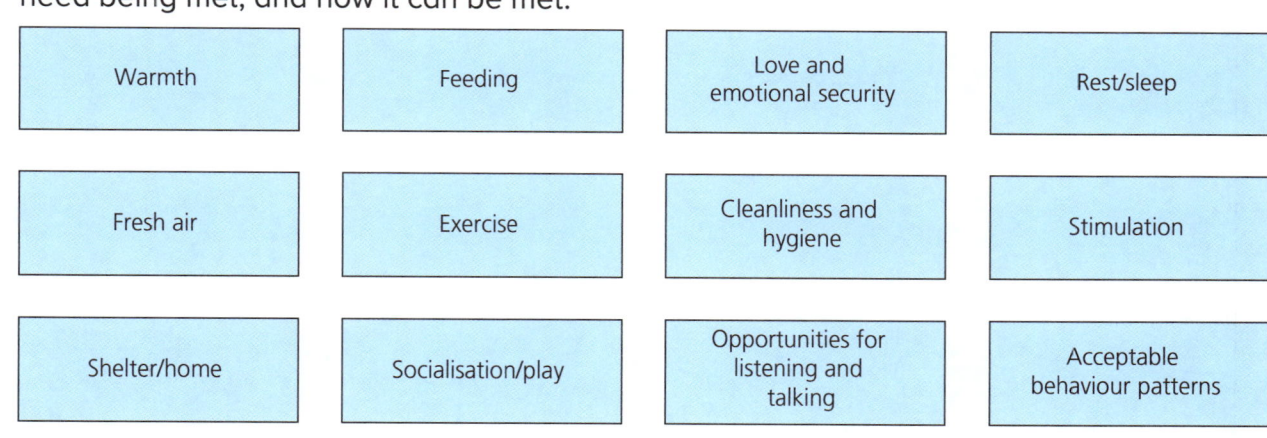

An example revision card is shown below.

Developmental need	Importance	How it is met
Stimulation	Develops curiosity and interests	Through making new friends, going to new places
	Meeting and playing with others broadens interests	Learning how to socialise with others
	Younger children enjoy new things, toys, songs, stories, finding them interesting	Interesting toys, books, activities and games

Developmental need	Importance	How it is met

Developmental need	Importance	How it is met

2 Create a spider diagram showing how **one** of the following activities can help children develop listening and talking skills and acceptable patterns of behaviour:

- going to the shops
- having a family meal
- going to the park.

> **Tip**
> Make sure that you are familiar with the developmental needs of children from birth to five years. You must be able to explain why they are important and give examples of how the needs can be met.

Topic Area 3: Postnatal checks, postnatal care and the conditions for development

3 Complete the summary chart below about the benefits of feeding routines for babies and children and another for parents and carers. Some parts have been completed for you.

Benefits for babies and children	Benefits for parents/carers
Bonding with parent/carer/siblings •	**Bonding** • develops the relationship with baby
Creates sense of security and belonging • feeding routine helps baby become part of family life; feels comfortable	**Relaxation and enjoyment** • enjoy time with baby, especially if breastfeeding, cannot do anything else
Learning routines around meal times •	**Regular meal times** •
Enjoyment •	**Interaction** • time for positive interaction between baby and carer; spending time with a child; may talk or sing to baby while feeding
Learning and development • parents/carers could talk to baby or child as she or he is feeding; this helps baby recognise voices and helps child to develop communication skills	**Nurturing** •

Short-answer exam-style practice questions

1 Identify **four** developmental needs of children, other than warmth and feeding.

  1 ....

  2 ....

  3 ....

  4 .... [4]

2 Give **two** examples of the importance of exercise for children.

  1 ....

  2 .... [2]

3 Give **two** examples of how children's need for exercise can be met.

  1 ....

  2 .... [2]

4 Identify **three** benefits for children of having a bath-time routine.

1 ....

2 ....

3 .... [3]

Long-answer exam-style practice questions

1 Discuss the importance of warmth for children and how the need for warmth can be met.

....

....

....

....

....

....

....

....

....

....

....

.... [6]

2 Mia has her six-week postnatal review with her health visitor. Describe examples of and give reasons for checks that would be carried out at this six-week review.

> **Plan your answer**
>
> **Question context and requirements**
> - The topic is the six-week postnatal check. You have to give examples of the checks carried out and reasons for those checks.
> - To check your knowledge, you could create a spider diagram of the checks and their reasons.
> - You could structure your answer by organising your information into paragraphs.
> - Try to write a Level 3 answer. This would include aspects such as:
>   – why the check is done at six weeks
>   – specific named examples of the checks – two or three of these
>   – examples of concerns the mother might have and questions she might ask
>   – examples of physical checks carried out and the reasons why.

Topic Area 3: Postnatal checks, postnatal care and the conditions for development

....
....
....
....
....
....
....
....
....
....
....
....
....
....
....
....
....
....
.... **[8]**

> ### Sample answer
>
> The health visitor will check that Mia is doing okay and coping with being a mum. If Mia had stitches or a caesarean, they will check that they are healing correctly. If Mia is having trouble coping with being a mum, she could have postnatal depression. This is common and can be helped. The health visitor may suggest that Mia goes to some new mum groups to meet other mums in a similar position. The health visitor may also check Mia's blood pressure to make sure she is doing okay physically.
>
> ### Review the sample answer
>
> - Use the mark scheme to mark this sample answer.
> - Is it a low-, medium- or high-level answer? How many marks did you give it, and why?
> - What can you suggest could be added to improve this answer?
> - How could organising the answer into paragraphs help to improve the answer?

Write a review of the sample answer here.

....
....
....
....

Mark scheme

Answer	Guidance
Reasons for postnatal review - To see how the mother is coping with the baby - Support for baby offered, e.g. breast/bottle feeding; baby routines - Mia will be asked how she is coping and feeling: depressed/tired, whether she might have postnatal depression; how she is bonding with baby - Guidance on exercise/physical activity/postnatal exercises, i.e. pelvic floor - Check Mia's physical health, mental health and well-being - Can discuss any concerns she may have about herself or her baby - Advice on contraception, on booking a smear test, on Mia's diet/weight loss/guidance on healthy eating **Checks carried out** - Any vaginal discharge - Breast check for lumps/mastitis/blocked milk ducts - Check uterus is going back to normal size - Diet checks: she might need supplements, e.g. iron/calcium - If Mia has had a period since giving birth - Incontinence/leaking urine - Leg check for varicose veins/swelling/symptoms to suggest a blood clot - Blood pressure taken - Pelvic exam: perineal check to see if stitches have healed, or if caesarean scar is healing - Check if suffering from constipation/haemorrhoids - Weight checked	**Level 3 checklist 6–8 marks** - Detailed description - Both checks and reasons provided - Relevant information - Use of appropriate terminology **Level 2 checklist 3–5 marks** - Sound description - Checks/reasons described – but not fully developed - Some relevant information - Uses some appropriate terminology **Level 1 checklist 1–2 marks** - Basic/limited description - Identification of checks or reasons only - List-like/muddled - Limited information - Uses some appropriate terminology

Topic Area 4: Childhood illnesses and a child-safe environment

4.1 Recognise general signs and symptoms of illness in children

Recall activities

1 Complete the words in the statements to explain the signs and symptoms of illness in children.

   o **Signs that a child is ill:** changes that occur when a child is becoming ill, for example, loss of app _ _ _ _ _ e, becoming 'clingy', irr _ _ _ _ le, continuous cr _ _ _ g, lethargic, qu _ _ ter than usual.

   o **Signs of illness:** conditions such as as v _ _ _ _ _ _ g, diarrhoea, high t _ _ _ _ _ _ _ _ _ e, breathing difficulties, fitting, developing a r _ _ h, becoming unresponsive.

> **Tip**
> To gain marks, you will need to know the signs and symptoms, and have examples of treatment, for each illness.
>
> To help you remember these facts, you could make a spider diagram for each illness showing its signs, symptoms and treatment.

2 Use the clues to fill in the crossword with names of different childhood illnesses.

ACROSS

1 A mild illness that often has a runny nose, sneezing and a sore throat. (4)
3 This illness can cause dehydration from vomiting and/or dehydration. (15)
4 The very sore throat associated with this illness can be soothed with lozenges or throat sprays. (10)

DOWN

1 The child may need to take an antihistamine tablet with this illness to calm the itchy rash. (7, 3)
2 An illness that manifests itself as a rash with small red/purple spots that don't fade when pressed with the side of a glass. (10)

3 Draw lines to match the illnesses with their signs, symptoms and treatments. The first one has been done for you.

Illness	Signs and symptoms	Treatment
Meningitis	Pain, swelling of the jaw in front of the ears, fever. Pain when eating and drinking.	Home care. Drink plenty of water to avoid dehydration. Rest, cut child's nails to prevent scratching. Use antihistamine lotion to ease itching.
Common cold	High fever, fretful, white spots inside mouth followed by blotchy rash on body. Discharge from eyes.	Home care, rest, drink plenty of fluids, give the child age-appropriate painkillers, apply warm or cold compress to swollen glands to reduc pain.
Gastroenteritis	Headache, fever, neck stiffness and joint pains, small red/purple spots that don't fade when pressed with the side of a glass. Inability to tolerate light, fits, very sleepy or difficult to wake.	Home care, rest, fluids. Take age-appropriate paracetamol or ibuprofen. A pharmacist can give advice and suggest treatments (lozenges, throat sprays).
Measles	Very sore throat, fever with temperature of 38°C or above, headache, earache, pain on swallowing, aches and pains in back and limbs.	Home care. Replace fluids with water or rehydrating remedy from pharmacist. If child is very young or if symptoms are severe or continue for more than 12 hours, see GP. Fluids only for 24 hours.
Chickenpox	Slight fever, red, itchy rash, child feels ill, severe headache.	Home care. Treat symptoms, i.e. headache, sore throat.
Tonsilitis	Sneezing, sore throat, running nose, headache.	GP will confirm diagnosis. Home care, damp cotton wool to clean the eyes. Age-appropriate paracetamol or ibuprofen to relieve fever. Plenty of fluids.
Mumps	Vomiting and diarrhoea; becoming dehydrated.	Take to hospital A&E/call 999 for emergency treatment – antibiotics, fluids, oxygen.

Topic Area 4: Childhood illnesses and a child-safe environment

Short-answer exam-style practice questions

1 Write a definition and an example of a **sign** of illness.

   ....

   .... [2]

2 State the meaning of **symptom**.

   .... [1]

3 Describe how you would care for a child with chickenpox.

   ....

   ....

   ....

   ....

   .... [4]

4 Identify **three** examples of symptoms that require emergency medical care.

   1 ....

   2 ....

   3 .... [3]

4.2 How to meet the needs of an ill child

Recall activities

1 Draw a line to match the needs of a sick child to the correct description.

Physical needs	These relate to the child's feelings.
Social needs	These relate to the child's thought processes such as thinking skills, understanding, learning and knowledge.
Emotional needs	These are related to the child's body.
Intellectual needs	These are related to a child's relationships with others.

> **Tip**
> Remember the different types of needs by the acronym **PIES**.
> **P** = Physical
> **I** = Intellectual
> **E** = Emotional
> **S** = Social

2 Complete the tables with a list of as many ways as you can to meet the needs of an ill child. 'Physical needs' has been completed for you.

Ways of meeting physical needs	Ways of meeting social needs
<ul><li>Ensure medication is taken as required.</li><li>Change dressings as required to improve comfort and to keep wounds clean</li><li>Provide plenty of fluids to drink; ensure the child is not dehydrated</li><li>Provide regular nutritional meals and include favourite foods, to restore appetite</li><li>Ensure an appropriate room temperature, not too hot or cold; provide blankets for warmth, to improve comfort levels and feelings of well-being</li><li>Open windows for fresh air or use an electric fan if it is too warm</li><li>Make sure the child gets enough sleep to help speed recovery</li><li>Give them help if needed, e.g. to sit up, to go to the toilet</li></ul>	<ul><li>Have a conversation, talking about the illness – how soon they will feel better, etc.</li></ul>
Ways of meeting intellectual needs	**Ways of meeting emotional needs**
<ul><li>Explain any medication or treatment and why it is necessary</li></ul>	<ul><li>Make sure they have their comfort blanket or favourite toy</li></ul>

Short-answer exam-style practice questions

1 State what PIES stands for.

.... [1]

2 State **three** examples of the emotional needs of an ill child.

1 ....

2 ....

3 .... [3]

Topic Area 4: Childhood illnesses and a child-safe environment

3 Identify **three** examples of the intellectual needs of an ill child.

   1 ....

   2 ....

   3 .... [3]

4 Identify **two** examples of how an ill child's social needs can be met.

   1 ....

   2 .... [2]

5 Identify **four** important physical needs of an ill child.

   1 ....

   2 ....

   3 ....

   4 .... [4]

6 Complete the table with the name of the correct illnesses listed below.

Mumps   **Measles**   **Meningitis**   **Tonsillitis**

Illness	Signs and symptoms
	• Sore throat and pain when swallowing • High temperature of 38°C or above • Headache • Earache • Back and limb pain
	• Headache • Fever • Stiff neck and joint pains • Small red/purple spots that do not fade when pressed with the side of a glass • Sensitive to light • Has fits • Very sleepy or difficult to wake
	• Swelling around jaw in front of ears • Fever • Eating and drinking is painful
	• High fever • White spots inside mouth, that is followed by blotchy rash on body • Eye discharge

[4]

4.3 How to ensure a child-friendly safe environment

Recall activities

1 Hazards around the house and garden are shown in the first column in each of the tables below.
   Complete the second column of each table to explain how each of these hazards can be prevented and children can be kept safe. An example answer has been added to each table for you.

Hazards in the kitchen	Prevention of kitchen hazards
<ul><li>Chemicals – bottles of detergent, bleach, cleaning materials – could be swallowed</li><li>Plug sockets – child might stick a knife or fingers in the socket</li><li>Sharp items – knives, cookie cutters could be in reach of a child</li><li>Lack of adult supervision</li><li>Drawers and cupboards – fingers could be trapped</li><li>Sharp corners can cause injury</li><li>Piles of plates and other crockery could fall and hurt the child</li><li>Hot pans on the cooker</li><li>Hot water/kettle – could be reached and pulled off worktop causing burns/scalding</li></ul>	<ul><li>Plug socket covers</li></ul>

Hazards in the toilet and/or bathroom	Prevention of toilet and/or bathroom hazards
<ul><li>Chemicals – bottles of detergent, bleach, cleaning materials – could be swallowed</li><li>Toiletries can be as poisonous as cleaning materials if swallowed</li><li>Water temperature – risk of scalding/burning</li><li>Hot taps</li><li>Young children in the bath – unsupervised – risk of drowning</li><li>Falls and slips on slippery surfaces</li><li>Unsafe bath toys – sharp edges, small parts</li></ul>	<ul><li>Toxic cleaning materials in a locked or high cupboard out of children's reach</li></ul>

Topic Area 4: Childhood illnesses and a child-safe environment

Stair hazards of stairs	Prevention of stair hazards of stairs
- Items left on the stairs could cause trips and falls - Carpets must not be loose - Children like exploring up the stairs but may fall - If there is a window near the stairs, a long curtain or blind with a long cord could cause a child to get tangled in cord or be strangled	- Young children must always be supervised on the stairs to avoid falls

Garden and play area hazards in gardens and play areas	Prevention of garden and play area hazards in gardens and play areas
- Insecure gates, sheds or fences – child could escape and be lost/harmed - Damaged play equipment - Equipment not being age appropriate – the child could fall from a great height - Play equipment not safe or assembled correctly - Poisonous plants in the garden if swallowed - Broken or uneven slabs on paths are a trip hazard - Ponds and water features – risk of drowning	- Sheds should be locked

2 Complete the road safety guidance with words from the list below.

reins   both   look   dangers   supervision   safe   hand

- Always cross on a zebra crossing or find a .... place to cross.
- Always hold the child's ....
- Children should be under the direct .... of an adult whenever crossing a road.
- Teach the child the Green Cross Code: stop, ..., listen.
- Teach the child to always look .... ways.
- Explain .... to the child and tell them about the risks.
- Use ....

3 Research the safety labels and find pictures of them.

Draw each of the safety symbols in the middle column of the chart below. The last one has been done for you.

Tip

You need to learn to recognise all the safety symbols and be able to explain their meaning.

Name of safety label	Label	Meaning
BSI kitemark		• The BSI Kitemark is a UK certification mark, administered by the British Standards Institution (BSI) as a symbol of safety and quality.
Lion mark		• This was introduced by the British Toy and Hobby Association. It is a recognisable consumer symbol denoting high standards of safety and quality.
UKCA		• The CE symbol is being phased out to be replaced by the UKCA symbol. It means the item has been safety tested and is the manufacturer's declaration that the item meets all toy safety requirements.
Age advice symbol		• This label identifies when toys or equipment are not suitable for children under the age of 36 months mainly displayed on toys that might not pass a 'choke' test and also used on products that have small parts that could be removed or swallowed.
Children's nightwear labelling	Low flammability To BS5722	• Children's nightwear must satisfy the flammability requirements specified in the British Standard 5722. • Babies' garments and adults' nightwear must carry a permanent label showing if they meet the Low Flammability Standard. This means the item is slow to burn.

Topic Area 4: Childhood illnesses and a child-safe environment

Short-answer exam-style practice questions

1 State the definition of a hazard.

   .... [1]

2 Identify **two** hazards found in a bathroom. Describe how the **two** hazards could be prevented.

   1 ....

   ....

   2 ....

   .... [4]

3 Suggest **two** ways that stairs could be made safe.

   1 ....

   .... [2]

4 State **three** road safety rules that children should be taught.

   1 ....

   2 ....

   3 .... [3]

5 Identify **three** ways that the age advice symbol protects children.

   1 ....

   2 ....

   3 .... [3]

Long-answer exam-style practice questions

Command verb practice

All of the questions asked will include a **command verb**. This tells you what you have to do to answer the question.

Examples of command verbs (in order of increasing difficulty) used in the longer, extended response, questions are shown and explained in the table below.

Command verb	Meaning
Describe	Give an account that includes all of the relevant facts, features or aspects of something
Explain	More depth and detail than a description. You will include relevant reasons for, purposes of, or effects of something
Analyse	You will separate information into components and examine it methodically and in detail, in order to explain and interpret it
Discuss	Give an account that considers a range of ideas and viewpoints
Justify	Give reasons to support your answer or conclusion
Evaluate	You will make a judgement about something by taking into account different factors and include strengths and weaknesses, or positives and negatives.

These longer, extended response questions are given either 6 or 8 marks. There will only be **one** 8-mark question and **two** 6-mark questions on the paper.

Exam technique

There is more to producing a good answer to an exam question than simply knowing the facts. The quality of your response, such as how you organise your answer and whether it is fully relevant to the question all help you to answer the question well.
- Read each question through carefully at least twice before you start your answer.
- Underline or highlight the command verb so that you are clear about what you have to do.
- Make sure the information given in your answer is accurate and relevant to the question – don't just write everything you know about a topic – answer the question you have been asked.

Topic Area 4: Childhood illnesses and a child-safe environment

1 Explain how parents can care for an ill child at home.

Plan your answer

Question context and requirements
- The topic is looking after an ill child at home.
- You have to give examples of how parents would provide care.
- Don't forget the 'PIES' needs of an ill child – make a list of ideas to respond to this.
- You could structure your answer by writing in paragraphs to organise your information – what will you write about in each paragraph?
- Read the mark scheme – aim to write a Level 3 answer. You need to:
  - include specific examples of ways to care for an ill child, with reasons
  - avoid writing much about the child's illness – this is not really relevant
  - focus your answer on what the parent should do, linked to PIES.

[8]

Review your answer
- Use the mark scheme to mark your answer – is it a high-level answer?
- Can you suggest anything extra you could have added?

Mark scheme

Answer	Guidance
How to care for an ill child at home: • Give child plenty of drinks/fluids • Lots of rest/sleep • Monitor child carefully/check temperature • Reassure child • Explain what is wrong with them • Child may want a lot of attention • Read stories/do play activities with child to distract them from illness • Give child any required (or prescribed) medicines such as painkillers, antibiotics, etc. Ensure child takes medication • Provide favourite toys • Light food should be offered, e.g. ice cream • Ensure there is fresh air/ventilation in the home **Explanations:** • Children need to keep hydrated when ill • Rest helps recovery/child will be tired • Explain what is wrong, so the child understands why they don't feel well • Keep child occupied/entertained/distracted – relieves boredom • Give child reassurance	**Level 3: 6–8 marks** • Detailed explanation • Specific ways of how to care for an ill child at home are given • Relevant information • Use of appropriate terminology **Level 2: 3–5 marks** • Sound explanation • One or more ways to care for an ill child at home are considered but not fully developed • Some relevant information • Uses some appropriate terminology **Level 1: 1–2 marks** • Basic explanation • May be a simple identification of ways to care for a sick child • Limited information • Uses little appropriate terminology

2 Describe ways that parents can make bath time enjoyable and safe for their child.

> **Plan your answer**
> **Question context and requirements**
> • You must give examples of 'ways' parents can make bath time enjoyable.
> • You must give examples of making bath time safe – refer to water, bath toys and temperature.
> • Don't just name the ways, describe them.
> • You could refer to aspects of development such as learning, enjoyment and bonding, for example, if you are aiming at a Level 3 answer.

....

....

....

....

....

....

Topic Area 4: Childhood illnesses and a child-safe environment

....

....

....

....

....

....

....

.... [8]

> **Review your answer**
> - Look through the mark scheme for this question.
> - How does your answer match up?
> - Mark your answer using the mark scheme.
> - What needs to be improved?

Mark scheme

Answer	Guidance
Safety: **Ensuring bath water temperature is not too hot:** • Put the cold water in first, test water temperature using elbow **Bath toy safety checks:** • Check for sharp edges, age advice label, Lion Mark, Kitemark, etc. **Enjoyment:** • **Helps child to sleep better** – warm water helps baby feel soothed, relaxed and ready to sleep • **Enjoyment** – fun games and bath toys, blowing bubbles; children look forward to this • **Learning and development** – exploring cause and effect when splashing; fine motor skills; hide and seek with toys; floating/sinking; vocabulary, singing, talking, getting used to being in water as preparation for swimming • **Bonding with parent/carer/siblings** – time spent playing together develops parent/child/sibling relationships • **Creates sense of security** – helps feelings of belonging; bathing routine helps baby become part of family life	**Level 3: 6–8 marks** • Detailed description of examples to create an enjoyable bath time • Specific ways safety checks are given • Relevant information • Use of appropriate terminology **Level 2: 3–5 marks** • Sound description of some examples • One or more ways to create enjoyable bath time at home are considered but not fully developed • Reference to safety • Some relevant information • Uses some appropriate terminology **Level 1: 1–2 marks** • Basic description • May be a simple identification of ways with little detail • Limited information – safety may not be mentioned • Uses little appropriate terminology

CAMBRIDGE NATIONAL
LEVEL 1/LEVEL 2

CHILD DEVELOPMENT

J809

EXAM PRACTICE WORKBOOK

Develop the vital skills you need to achieve the best results possible in your Cambridge National Child Development exams, with this expert-written Exam Practice Workbook.

Written by an experienced author, this write-in Exam Practice Workbook:
- helps you to remember and retrieve information with a range of recall activities for every topic area
- reinforces your understanding and boosts your exam confidence with both short-answer and extended-response exam-style practice questions for you to try and activities that help you to break down the question, plan and review the answer
- allows you to work through on your own either in class or at home, or for last-minute revision.

Includes:
- Recall activities – crosswords, quizzes and more
- Hints and tips on exam technique
- Scaffolded exam-style practice questions
- Example student answers

Also available:

9781398351202 Level 1/Level 2 Cambridge National in Child Development (J809): Second Edition

9781398351196 My Revision Notes: Level 1/Level 2 Cambridge National in Child Development: Second Edition

 HODDER Education
+44 (0)1235 827827
education@hachette.co.uk
www.hoddereducation.com

ISBN 978-1-3983-8485-9

MIX
Paper | Supporting responsible forestry
FSC™ C104740

Every effort has been made to trace all copyright holders, but if any have been inadvertently overlooked, the Publishers will be pleased to make the necessary arrangements at the first opportunity.

Although every effort has been made to ensure that website addresses are correct at time of going to press, Hodder Education cannot be held responsible for the content of any website mentioned in this book. It is sometimes possible to find a relocated web page by typing in the address of the home page for a website in the URL window of your browser.

Hachette UK's policy is to use papers that are natural, renewable and recyclable products and made from wood grown in well-managed forests and other controlled sources. The logging and manufacturing processes are expected to conform to the environmental regulations of the country of origin.

Orders: please contact Hachette UK Distribution, Hely Hutchinson Centre, Milton Road, Didcot, Oxfordshire, OX11 7HH. Telephone: +44 (0)1235 827827. Email education@hachette.co.uk Lines are open from 9 a.m. to 5 p.m., Monday to Friday. You can also order through our website: www.hoddereducation.co.uk

ISBN: 978 1 3983 8485 9

© Judith Adams 2023

First published in 2023 by
Hodder Education (a trading division of Hodder & Stoughton Limited),
An Hachette UK Company
Carmelite House
50 Victoria Embankment
London EC4Y 0DZ

www.hoddereducation.co.uk

The authorised representative in the EEA is Hachette Ireland, 8 Castlecourt Centre, Dublin 15, D15 XTP3, Ireland (email: info@hbgi.ie)

Impression number   10 9 8 7 6 5

Year   2027 2026 2025

All rights reserved. Apart from any use permitted under UK copyright law, no part of this publication may be reproduced or transmitted in any form or by any means, electronic or mechanical, including photocopying and recording, or held within any information storage and retrieval system, without permission in writing from the publisher or under licence from the Copyright Licensing Agency Limited. Further details of such licences (for reprographic reproduction) may be obtained from the Copyright Licensing Agency Limited, www.cla.co.uk

Cover photo © marseus – stock.adobe.com

Illustrations by Integra Software Services Pvt. Ltd, Pondicherry, India

Typeset by Integra Software Services Pvt. Ltd, Pondicherry, India

Printed and Bound in Great Britain by Bell & Bain Ltd, Glasgow

A catalogue record for this title is available from the British Library.